"In a vast and sweeping poem, Zev Levinson offers us a bold song from the frontiers of all waters and species, living and dead, to 'build a bridge from grief.' Risky and full of heart, these words of loss and joy ring with a mythic quality that summons native spirits—Karuk, Yurok, Hupa, Sinkyone and Wiyot—as well as the voices of such poets as Whitman, Coleridge and Ginsberg. We enter another realm bridging fish eggs among school desks and redwood hymns, calling forth the sanctity of the forest. Written outside of time among brethren druid trees, Levinson's playful, grand and profound poem-song (a tribute to both his father and to his mentor Guy, everyman) moves from outpost ghosts to a leaf pitched in a waterfall to an insect on the smallest tree—a benediction to hold and restore mysteries."

    —Susan G. Wooldridge, author of *poemcrazy: freeing your life with words*

"This is a quirky lifework poem with a coherent and positive vision of possibility in the face of loss. It is a truly beautiful piece about the sorrow and goodness of Californians in redwood country, and as part of it being about goodness, it evokes wonderful practical things that people can do to make the world better: write poetry, fix trails, teach poetry, remember, relax, let go, love, get older on bicycles in the fog by marshes, even while the economic drama of the country and the state changes some things, but leaves some things recognizable—all in Levinson's rootsy and updated romantic idiom because Levinson needs a language commensurate with his unarmored joy.

It's as if poetry lets people go back a bit and forward at the same time to get things right for us now. The photos all suggest questions about who is watching this scene. By way of an answer, this poem enacts the creation of a fabulist, healthy point of view of a flower-vendor poet in Arcata turned teacher-poet in the schools, a figure that emerges like a John Clare shepherd and a large-souled character out of Whitman. And there are many wonderful lines in it like 'You know the fauna watches you.' The fauna were also watching Wallace Stevens."

    —David Blair, author of *Arsonville* and *Friends with Dogs*

SONG OF SIX RIVERS

ZEV LEVINSON

Song of Six Rivers

Published by Humboldt State University Press
HSU Library
1 Harpst Street
Arcata, CA 95521-8299
hsupress@humboldt.edu

Publisher's Cataloging-in-Publication Data
Names: Levinson, Zev, 1966-
Title: Song of Six Rivers / by Zev Levinson.
Description: First trade paperback original edition. | Arctata [California]: Humboldt
State University Press, 2018. | Includes listing of historical photograph references & links
to HSU's Humboldt Room archive collection.
Identifiers: LCCN 2017950632 | ISBN-10: 1-947112-02-3 (pbk.) | ISBN-13:
978-1-947112-02-5 (pbk.)
Subjects: Poetry—21st century. | Prose poems, American. | Humboldt Bay
(Calif.)—Poetry. | Six Rivers National Forest (Calif.)--Poetry. | Humboldt County
(Calif.)--Poetry. Classification: PS3523.E7995 S66 2017

Interior design, layout and editing by CM Phillips & Ashley Schumann
Cover Design by CM Phillips & Jennifer Rand

Set in Adobe Garamond type

Dedicated to Guy Kuttner, 1946-2011
Grateful inspiration from "Kingfisher" by Michael Bickford

Preface

Guy knew it would be our last conversation. I did not. Was it just my naïveté, or reluctance to confront another loss? I had left a message: "Is there anything I can do to help?" He returned my call and sounded perfectly fine and in good spirits, having bounced back after suddenly nearing death, a rare disease throwing him down hard at age sixty-four.

When we first met at the Redwood Writing Project's retreat for teachers, Guy, his wife Cindy, and I had immediately felt kinship. Guy Kuttner seemed more comfortable with himself than anyone I had ever known. He was effusive and gregarious while grounded in a core of compassion, meeting your eyes with a gentle intensity. Bits of songs were naturally woven into his dialogue. Playfully serious, Guy was uncompromising when it came to teaching and to nourishing the heart, protecting the environment, and waging peace.

One summer, before we departed from the retreat, Bob Sizoo, its founder, called a meeting. Funding for the retreat had dried up and teachers could no longer receive aid to participate. He proposed that we change the nature of the event and have attendees pay to experience a week of workshops with published authors. Several of us were game, and we tried the new format for a few years with a great deal of effort and not enough signups. Most of our meetings were held in Guy and Cindy's cozy living room. All along, Guy reminded us that we should only be doing this if it was a pleasure and not too much work. Eventually, he suggested we just rent Camp Mattole as a collective of equals who wanted to craft their writing and spend good time together, maybe even turn it into a retreat for all kinds of artists.

The year we agreed to stop hiring paid presenters and to relax the overall format, Guy succumbed to the illness, vanishing from our world within a few winter weeks. As I joined hundreds of people at his memorial in the local grange for hours of storytelling and music, I finally understood how deeply he had affected our community. His gift to our writing group remains six years later: the Lost Coast Writers Retreat, a sanctuary where writers become more who they are as they immerse themselves in their creative work and in the Mattole River, both alone and in the company of the tribe.

One of the places where his ashes were scattered was the group's favorite swimming hole. I don't know why, but I was the first to step into the water and release from my cupped hands the white particles to the wind and the river on that overcast day. I felt a responsibility fall upon me to keep his legacy alive, his generosity and message of peace as a teacher, activist, and believer in a sacred, sustainable earth.

At the same time, I was nearing fifty and asking myself what I would someday leave behind. I had always wondered if I entirely faced the reality—or unreality—of my father's death. Dad had left a significant legacy, having been a community leader, professor, cantor, and stand-in rabbi for a synagogue in need. He was so beloved and esteemed that a thousand people attended his funeral. Of course, he meant more than all that to me: he was my role model and in our closest moments he felt like the ultimate friend. But a car accident splintered my family, hurling Dad into a four-month coma until a simple cold was more than his impaired immune system could take. It was for the best that he didn't survive, so extreme had been the damage. It was not for the best that modern medicine enabled him to linger until one day my mother told him that we would be okay and that he could let go. He died the next day. I was fourteen.

Ever since reaching adulthood, I have questioned if I have been living to my fullest, if the trauma has kept me from my true potential. Was my past keeping me from achieving a clear vision of the present? I was tested three years after Guy's death when I began writing *Song of Six Rivers* at Camp Mattole and found my father unexpectedly walking into the poem. He was with me more than usual in those days, since I was starting to edit the third edition of his book, *The Jews in the California Gold Rush*. That very summer, my mother had asked me to help bring out this next edition. She helps steer the Commission for the Preservation of Pioneer Jewish Cemeteries and Landmarks in the West, which had published the first two editions and which my father helped found. The entire Commission wanted this one to come out now. My poem was supposed to deal with the loss of one man, not two. I didn't know if I could do justice to both of them.

It had taken me decades to even read my father's book. I had given myself poor excuses such as its being dry history, but the truth was that it was just too close to the fiber of my being. I would often weep when I listened to recordings of Dad's voice; what would it be like to read his carefully wrought ideas? When I finally sat down with the paperback second edition—the first, in hardcover, still on my shelf and bearing his inscription to me, *With love, From Dad*—I could hear his voice saying every sentence. This caused me to read very slowly, wanting to absorb every trace. But it hurt like nothing else ever had. Could I burrow into this new project and become even more intimate with his words as I pored over them and kept on hearing his voice? Would it be the last time I would hear him? As I began to edit, and to write about Guy, the inevitability of Dad's mortality and absence forced its way into the poem. Yet working on his book would not just be an honor, it would be the first time I could collaborate with my father.

Because this was the first digital scan of the text, what I thought might be a yearlong endeavor stretched into three years. My family, and others, grew impatient, wondering if they would see the publication in their lifetimes. The happy outcome, however, at least to my way of seeing things, is that my father's book and this one are being published almost simultaneously. Both that exacting editing process—during which I eventually allowed myself to have long conversations with my father as I read and reread his language—and saying what I needed to in this poem, have helped me reconcile my losses.

The poem was composed and recomposed over some years, partly because of its length, but also because of suggestions from my literary family at the Lost Coast Writers Retreat, and from Jim Dodge who was willing to look at an early draft. Jim recommended the rhyme scheme that I settled on. Among a number of his other suggestions was to find a more apt title than what I had previously chosen, one that better reflected the watershed and natural landscape rather than lines drawn arbitrarily on maps. Our discussion traveled into delightfully arcane terrain, involving percentages of biotic shift when determining ecosystem boundaries, and etymologies of words in the poem. Bob Sizoo found the right title during last winter's retreat at his home in Oregon.

Six rivers of thanks flow to the enthusiastic, efficient team at Humboldt State University Press: Kyle Morgan, who wanted to publish the poem and had the vision of an illustrated edition; CM Phillips, my ingenious friend who headed the design and edits of the book, guided me through the seas of publication, and suggested I provide the context of the poem in a preface; and Ashley Schumann, who assisted in the whole process and who, with CM, combed through more than twelve thousand historic photographs from HSU's archives to find the perfect images, and helped with the layout. Martin Swett and Thomas B. Dunklin enhanced the project with their timeless photography, giving me new lenses to perceive this land and water. Jennifer Rand deserves her own river of thanks for not only knowing the way of the current, but navigating and soothing my turbulent waters, co-designing the book cover, and insisting that this preface be as clear as the Mattole. I'll always be thanking Guy for his inspiration. His final words to me were *I love you*. Before hanging up, I replied *I love you too*. The line is still open.

Lev Levinson

February 2017
Bend, Oregon, Winter Retreat
Lazy Rockin' Double-bar BS Mini-ranchette and Retired Educator Care Farm

MOUTH OF LITTLE RIVER.

Humboldt Co., California.

For additional copies

The elder poets close their books
And turn in time to alder white.
Though some remain another page,
Prepare to bid them all goodnight.
Their voices shroud and husk my dreams.
Still waiting here? they grimly say,

Their faces gaunt and earthen-lined.
I've squandered strength on sun, on play.
The sun will catch our eyes and hopes.
Those mostly content slowly melt,
Uncoiling dreams gone unregained—
Sigh gratitude for sparks they felt.

Yet those who wonder why we're here
Stand restless, relentless, seeking more,
And veering from the daily course
They gaze upon a distant shore.
Old poets wed the setting sun,
Enough of watching whelps at play.

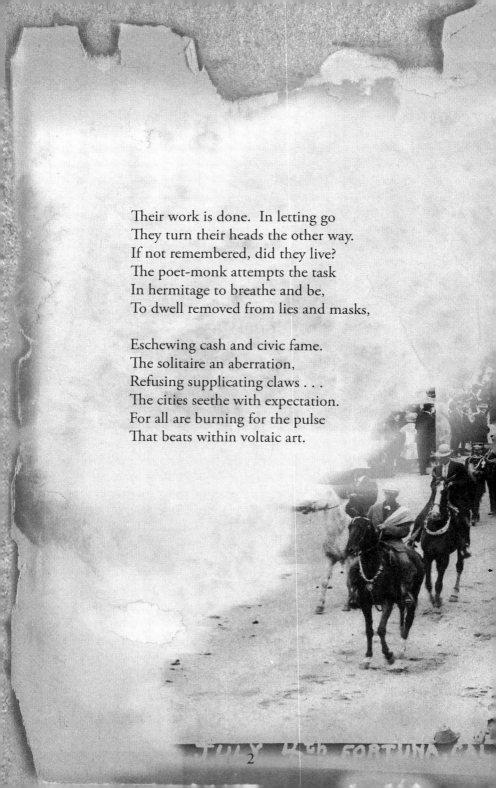

Their work is done. In letting go
They turn their heads the other way.
If not remembered, did they live?
The poet-monk attempts the task
In hermitage to breathe and be,
To dwell removed from lies and masks,

Eschewing cash and civic fame.
The solitaire an aberration,
Refusing supplicating claws . . .
The cities seethe with expectation.
For all are burning for the pulse
That beats within voltaic art.

KEIR FORTUNA Nº 3002

3

But what am I to paint or write,
Oh hermitage within my heart?
One missing poet calls to me,
A message that I must deliver,
For in Guy's name I breathe this world,
Remember ashes on the river.

He keeps on singing on this wind
As I absorb the heat and light,
Insisting that the song remain
As wild as my own birthright.
Keep on sounding, Zev, he sings.
Your teachings more than bread and butter

Shall travel through the veins of children,
Instill the passion offspring utter.
You've taken in our sublime sphere,
You've journeyed all throughout our lands,
Partaking daily from the source,
Restoring poems to our hands.

You've sojourned here these fifteen years
Above my sacred swimming hole,
Held close by tribal brethren
Immersed in the mystery of the Mattole
Where Clear-Water spirits sparkle code,
Yet doubt you can translate this voice.

FISHING FOR
STEELHEAD
FERNBRIDGE

Why, ancient memory and this moment
Shall hush your snibbly inner noise.
The seismic breath Petrolian,
The magma beneath Honeydew,
The treachery of Panther Gap,
Whose ice-paths mirror Xanadu.

You've seen snow fall upon these sands
And heard Cordelia's youthful chant
Echoing beyond the mound of skulls . . .
Do you recall this illuminant?
Her Sunday sauna purged your core
As Doctor Nash, the healer-scribe,

Beside the Mattole laid you bare—
Their words, their wine you did imbibe.
As Guy laughs out this terrestrial list,
So Cindy bears toward our fingers
His books, his drum, and his guitar,
Entrusting legacy should linger.

But why stop here? laughing still—
This howling coastline, take it slow.
All such loam be your frontier
As far as Cape Mendocino.
Confront the chimera of Capetown,
From fire-breathing Wildcat Ridge,

Tectonic Ferndale Cemetery
Disrupts the crossing of Fernbridge.
These grounds have made you more complete.
Oh, sing! and with me harmonize.
Deep in this song we both survive:
Now this terrain immortalize.

Our lucent Mattole reveals the scheme,
Almost silent, just a sliver,
Till I anoint with all the waters,
Adopt the skin of all six rivers.
On days this lorn Jen takes my hand,
Understanding when I cry,

Reminding me of veiled truths
And urging me to speak of Guy.
My father davens to these words,
These canticles borne from our bed.
He's hovered thirty-four long years,
Expecting message-texts gone dead.

Destroy the decades' decadence!
A chorus builds and I head south.
Dispelling ghosts with cobweb minds,
I follow salmon to the mouth.
All species singing, mountains moan
Until the earth is made anew.

With redwoods sprung from molten speech,
All trees unfurling what is true
That deer and quail receive as blessings,
A grandeur of this forest vast
Releasing crystal elixirs
Wrought unperceived in aeons past.

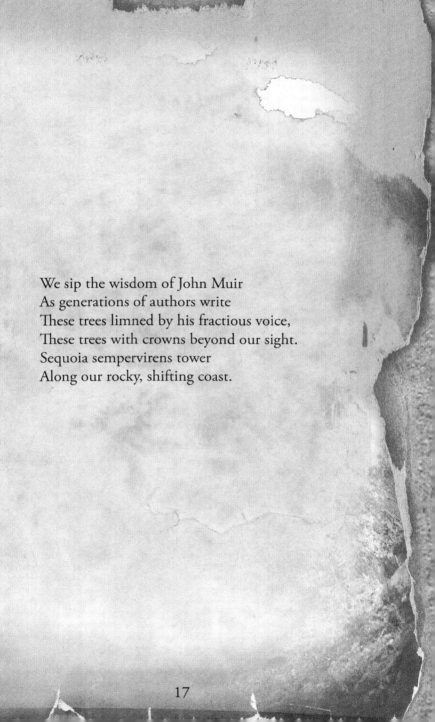

We sip the wisdom of John Muir
As generations of authors write
These trees limned by his fractious voice,
These trees with crowns beyond our sight.
Sequoia sempervirens tower
Along our rocky, shifting coast.

COLLAR TREE ON OVERLAND ROAD, HUMBOLDT C
TO BY KEIR, FORTUNA, CAL.   No 1304.

18

Sequoiadendra gigantea
Loom until we feel lost.
Metasequoia glyptostroboides
Transplanted from the Chinese shores
As graceful as the dawn on dew
Remind us to fling wide our doors.

Such shadow-casting ancient beings
Are as the roiling blue Pacific,
And if I grasp for any essence
Of moments flashing and specific,
I find impossible the task,
As opened moments steal my thoughts

Till I become another mote
With millions in a sunbeam caught
Who dance among these endless forms:
Sword ferns that frame scintillant whales,
A mountain lion asleep in sorrel,
Banana slugs, and foxes' trails

All leading from my brain to heart . . .
Diversity eludes compare,
Enfolds and frees this laden soul,
And renders me at last *aware*.
Aware and awake, I heave my howl
While Yurok drift into the mist,

Gold dust debasing noble visage.
At Whitey's Gulch, sage Liz insists
She's seen the albino silhouette
And heard the medicine man's chant
Across the vale from Katamin
Where deerskinned Karuk proudly danced.

A discrete shape has lumbered past—
The locals cringe as something shrieks,
A beast, some say, that has no name,
But others claim they hear it speak.
The children of these broken tribes,
Still mourning countless crooked losses,

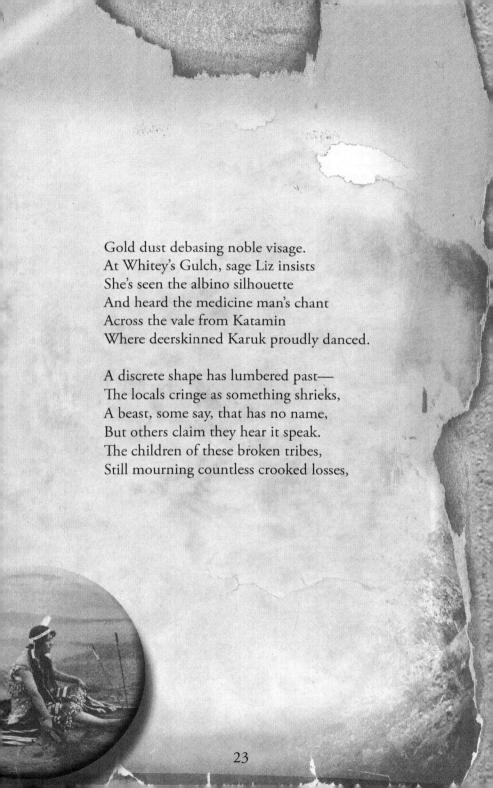

A glimpse of the coast California
A. W. Ericson, photographer

They look to me for unearthed poems
And bear their totems by church crosses.
Can all this naming be enough?
These poems all I have to give.
Will they hold as lasting proof,
Imperative why I have lived?

The Hupa and the Sinkyone
Upon these vital lands did reign,
Whose villages were burned and torn,
Whose kin fought only to be slain.
I've hearkened to the Wiyot songs,
Helped restore mysteries as I can;

I've eaten from their hidden gardens;
No longer dream utopian.
Some dynasties shall walk no more.
There is no way we can appease
Those spirits without resting place,
Nor end the nightmare, make it cease.

Such prayers as could cleave the clouds
I wing unto those hearts of sorrow—
Salute the sun of future days,
Compose a song meant for tomorrow.
Though rains diminish and oceans rise,
I pray new storms would someday cleanse

All thought of reaping recompense,
The message that the spilled blood sends.
For we remember otherwise
And pray these rivers fill again.
Rain seeped into our very dreams,
Humming down for weeks on end,

Absorbed into the evergreens,
Dripping deep through memory.
Thirty days nonstop, it was said,
So canyoned creeks did rush the sea.
Behind this redwood curtain, rain:
Those rhythms soaking through our roofs

(EK2)RIO DELL, CALIF.,Dec 23---Bridge Out---
Highway 101 bridge is out at the town of Rio Dell
28 miles south of Eureka, as the Eel River takes

29

RAIN DAMPENED CLOTHES, BUT NOT SPIRITS, BIG BRIDGE CELEBRATION, NOV. 16, 1911. KEIR PHOTO

Drove home that we had found a home
And offered lasting liquid proof
In spite of all, we'd settled here,
So far from San Francisco Bay,
A world rich with reverie—
Old friends, our families, far away.

The interweaving redwood fog
Increased the storms and swelling squalls;
Informed the fabric of our brains
And permeated poor-built walls.
This rain defined our days and nights—
This wet defined the earth and sky.

Like hematite we cast a sheen,
We wondered, could life ever dry?
So we became as salamanders—
Among the roots we took our ease
Ensconced within humistic mulch,
Hence heard the brethren druid trees.

And as clouds finally dissipate
We yearn to venture out once more,
And gusting gales in course subside,
Come see what lies beyond our door.
Come, gather all, explore the light;
Come, gather gear for time afield.

Then sing the humble shire clear!
Then let the magic be revealed.
Our Sanctuary Forest beckons,
Where stalwart stewards plead for parcels,
Where greed is barely beyond reach,
Where virgin stands remain mere morsels.

Indeed one slips outside of time—
It's here in quiet solitude
That one can cradle inner peace,
A Southern Humboldt interlude
Between the madness and the jolt,
Just contemplation, ecstasy.

So simple the old miracle:
The formula: to breathe and be.
In arcane enclaves, farmers' fields,
The art of living catches fire.
Lone sculptor in his seaside cabin
Shapes wood to form a winter's pyre.

Stroll beach of black sands, Shelter Cove;
Taste Briceland berries jammed in jars;
Survey the black bear foraging;
Long Whitethorn nights, with white-torn stars.
That groove of Garberville goes deep,
Exposed to the thrum of 101.

Now loudly buzzing, yet somehow chill,
Bad Harleys rev the Redwood Run.
Along the Giants' Avenue
Roam tourists, a distant kin,
Absorbing verdant global science—
In awe, they touch sequoia skin,

While innocents from anywhere
Do find themselves on limbs so high,
That here they dwell to climb higher,
Recall Julia Butterfly.
And vagabonds who search for work,
To trim fat plants for months on end,

HOTEL SEQUOIA

Lurk under bridges until then
In hopes of hoard to smoke and tend.
Hear Reggae on the River pump
As summer solstice royalty
With blood gone feral—true out-law—
Sit back and sip their magic tea.

Soon all regard their watersheds,
Give name to what they know they feel,
Destroyed or restoring the source,
Two rivers' portmanteau: Mateel.
South fork of Eel down through Benbow
Where I tally spawning Chinook—

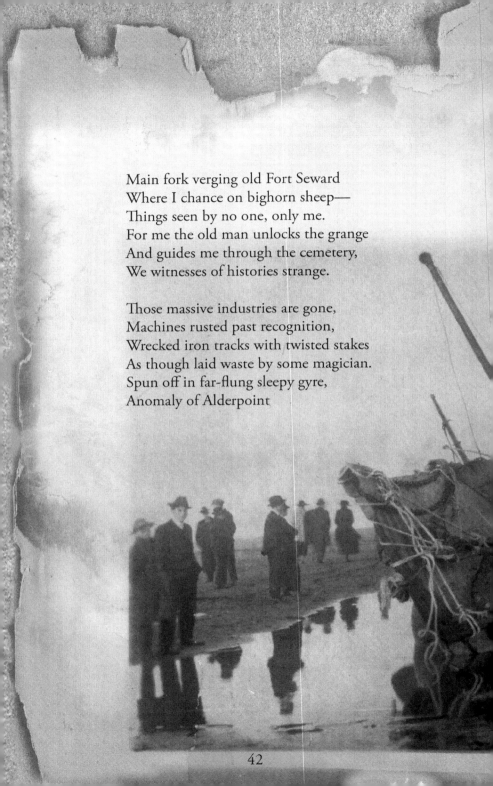

Main fork verging old Fort Seward
Where I chance on bighorn sheep—
Things seen by no one, only me.
For me the old man unlocks the grange
And guides me through the cemetery,
We witnesses of histories strange.

Those massive industries are gone,
Machines rusted past recognition,
Wrecked iron tracks with twisted stakes
As though laid waste by some magician.
Spun off in far-flung sleepy gyre,
Anomaly of Alderpoint

U.S. Submarine
Samoa Beach
Humbolat Co. Cal
Freeman Art Co.

43

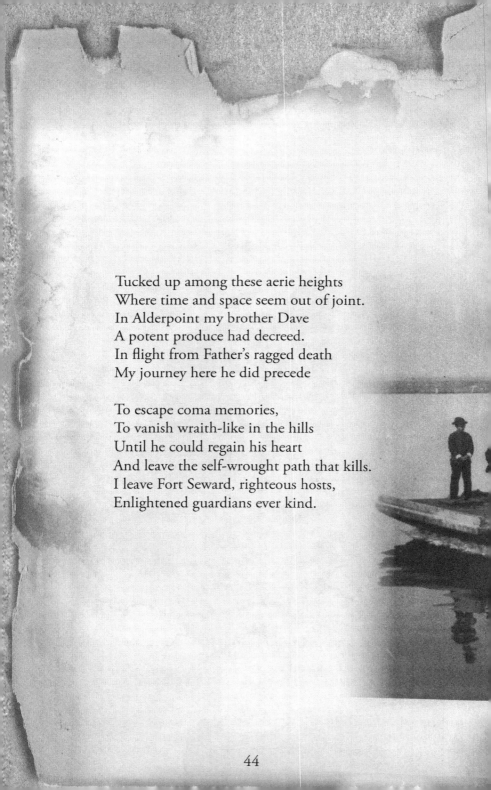

Tucked up among these aerie heights
Where time and space seem out of joint.
In Alderpoint my brother Dave
A potent produce had decreed.
In flight from Father's ragged death
My journey here he did precede

To escape coma memories,
To vanish wraith-like in the hills
Until he could regain his heart
And leave the self-wrought path that kills.
I leave Fort Seward, righteous hosts,
Enlightened guardians ever kind.

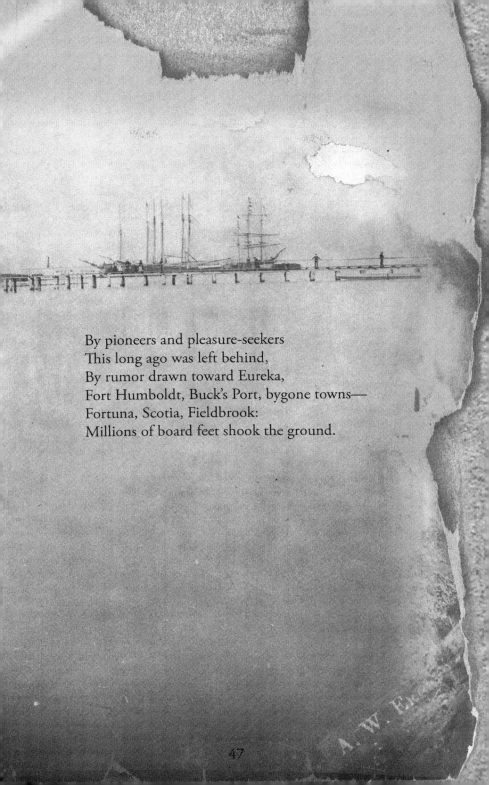

By pioneers and pleasure-seekers
This long ago was left behind,
By rumor drawn toward Eureka,
Fort Humboldt, Buck's Port, bygone towns—
Fortuna, Scotia, Fieldbrook:
Millions of board feet shook the ground.

Rohnerville, McKinleyville,
Miranda, Redway, Rio Dell:
These places build my destiny.
I sing their schools, I know them well.
It was SalMan, Murphy School,
Who brought me back, year after year,

(Who hatched fish eggs amidst the desks),
Until I finally learned to hear
That this is why I'm given verse
To sing to children who have sprung
From generations of those mills,
That they will carry forth the song.

The Van Duzen has lost its voice.
In Pamplin Grove and Grizzly Creek
Warm algae blooms in siphoned water,
In sad trickles no more deep.
In skyward Hydesville and Carlotta
We heed the eerie call of owls;

To Bridgeville, lonesome latitude,
We fathom why coyotes howl.
The city lights and television
Play tricks on the historian—
Eureka dreams of modernism
While steeped in things Victorian.

It's hard to parse in such dense fog
The drunken rants heard in the Shanty.
Old sea dogs gathered in the Snug
Once huddled 'round their heated brandy—
This chill that slinks beneath the clothes,
The thickest wool it sets beneath,

-Arcata Fair- 1919-

Swirling in wreaths, obscuring sight,
It gnaws at bones, and rattles teeth.
Yea, fog writhes through the myriad marshes,
And biking past in nightmare cold
The body's swathed in sodden cloak,
Benumbed, forsaken, small, and old.

Eureka's and Arcata's commerce
Once pushed my tricycle up hills,
Blue conveyance of bundled flowers
Pleased senses as plain vases filled.
But that was in a distant time,
And now more lore, now less muscle—

Though hardly filling needed coffer—
Bouquets of words I gladly hustle.
If gentrified these days, less hip,
Arcata holds the pulse and hum,
The hippie vibe enduring yet;
So I grow old but abide young.

Hot chai in hand, content to sit—
The pastel sky on pastel buildings—
There on my bench and soak it in,
The plaza, my pen wielding.
I've lived in Arcata throughout time.
The rhythm as the cattle tear

At grass, as though a coded poem,
In silent farmland ocean air;
The waves that crash along the shore
And beat at sculpted shifting dunes;
The crowd, brass band at baseball games;
The fire siren wailing *Noon!*

Sharp wind that trills against the wires,
The wind and sun that whisk away
Throughout the rocking redwood peaks
The symbiotic fog of gray
That haunts the redwood canopy.
For I have heard that redwoods sing,

In search of lifeblood's fog and rain,
A song that from the sky will bring
Such rain as carries on for days,
Erasing warmth of truant sun—
Until grasshopper's clearing chant
Brings back the light: the sun by song.

Then redwoods start their hymn again,
And if you stay here long enough
And stand beneath that urgent rain
And watch the flora in wind move,
Then trees and insects hum more sense,
You know the fauna watches you,

Till all your sins have vaporized;
And know your deathless days are few.
The summer wind blows ardent, quick,
Straight up the skirt of 14th Street.
I pause to read the tombstone dates
In this wind defying the heat

And contemplate the thin border
Between those bodies in the ground
And ours, with Farmers Market yield—
Our souls' procession flows through town.
Alive in celebration bright:
North Country Fair, dancing bodies,

Deft drumming music promulgates
Naked plazoid hippie hotties.
Another home I was ensconced:
Twelve years gone by in Freshwater.
Next door my landlord slowly died.
Ten years of bliss; the rest, disaster.

In isolation roses bloomed:
Freshwater of the woodland walks:
I tended trails, slashing branches,
And I arranged a thousand rocks
To stem erosion in the rain;
And building bridges over creeks

Entered the spirit of the forest
Where I did walk six hundred weeks.
Above the valley I would roam
To Kneeland, Greenwood Heights I'd pass
Toward far sun-brewed Maple Creek,
I left behind skies overcast.

Cows on the road; towering crags;
Red-tailed hawks' cries arrow the air;
El Rio Loco by Korbel;
In Blue Lake pints of crafted beer.
Over Lord-Ellis, Berry Summits,
We raised the yurt, straw-bale house—

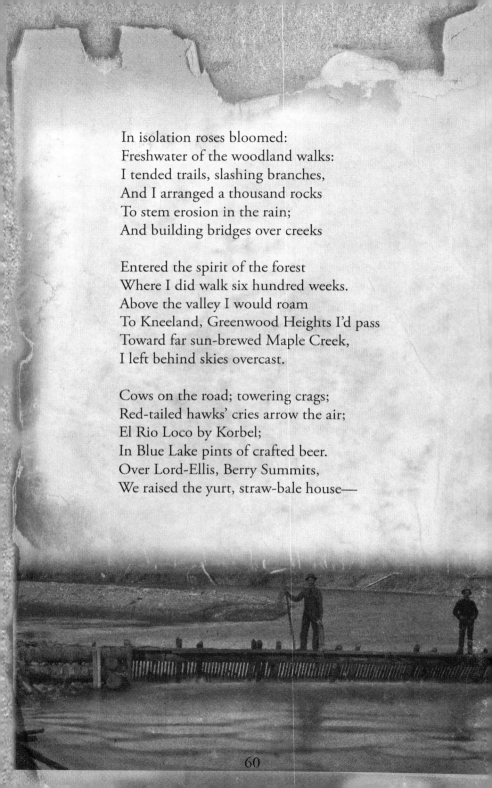

Weitchpec Post Office 1919

Weitchpec

62

In dreams the land was named Gondwoot:
Reality diaphanous.
Long summer days in Willow Creek,
On rafts upon the Trinity
Till joining with the sacred Klamath,
Embattled, dammed fragility.

The Hoopa realm, both wild and tamed,
Refracts memories blessed and sad,
As genocide wrought anywhere
Erupts from appetite gone mad.
Across Weitchpec from times unknown,
It's said how simple life could be

If we could but awareness hone
Beyond gold-mine economy.
The meat is smoked, the prayers sung,
So far from law, far from the hate
That emanated from those ships
That sailed through the Golden Gate.

Continue on, ocean beckons,
The kayak headed for the coast—
Great Spirit touching those devout
When passing frontier outpost ghosts.
Trees of true mystery call to me,
And headlong, heartlong, surging deep—

A leaf pitched in a waterfall—
It is here forever I could sleep.
So placed beneath Ilúvatar
That I might see my time is brief—
An insect on the tallest tree—
I must—yes—build a bridge from grief.

In Fern Canyon I hear whispers
As maiden-fronds release the seep.
By unseen fingers I am brushed.
What secrets will this old heart keep?
An elk drinks from the raining drips—
He leads me seaward, past his herd,

And I approach, as in a dream,
Where from the tides I hear one word.
One word of summons. One word: *Sing!*
Guy's voice, his figure, on the waves.
In purest tones I hear this word,
His face so in my mind engraved.

His kayak moves within the mist,
Careening to the four lagoons,
And I pursue through serpent surf
Until at length I importune
That he might lead me to the nexus,
The words that spawn a difference—

Abiding words I would transmit
To unborn generations hence.
Our kayaks skim the Moonstone rocks;
So through the spray our vessels race,
Until I'm torn from compass points,
Until unmoored from time and space.

Blurred minutes, hours, days go by.
The begging of my weary soul
I must refuse, I must deny
To stop at the mouth of the Mattole,
For there the river gushes forth:
My quarry leaves me far behind

A Warm Day.

In turning inland from the shore.
Despair now renders me half blind,
And yet I know where I must go,
Which bend I finally need to turn,
The only way to unlock life—
I know my grief I must unlearn,

For death withholds insistent sap.
My spirit guide is in all things
If just this heart could recognize,
And this is why I hear him sing.
I churn as though a centrifuge,
Arriving at the hallowed place;

Undone, collapse where we first met,
The ending of my frenzied chase.
By sands where we once spoke and laughed,
By sands our tribe scattered his ash,
The water breaks in crystal shards:
A mighty salmon rises, flashes,

A vision in the pristine pool,
Its scales hurling back the sun,
Its motion battering my senses,
Pulling me from my skeleton.
It disappears into the river
As a wind that stirs the leaves

And sends the trees to sudden swaying
Aims my heart toward belief.
Then from the trees an airborne dart,
A forest sound, a streak of blue,
An image I remember well—
Kingfisher, kingfisher, is that you?

Embodied in a shape with wings,
This tufted bird a sign of Guy
Settles on a nearby branch
And pierces me with quizzical eye,
My body now electrified.
This totem of the man I knew,

Who lit the way that I could follow,
This signals that my quest is true.
I merge with Guy in holy bond.
We are of bird, and of fish,
We are of ventures of this world,
A sky and ocean synthesis.

From darkness reaching toward the light,
We of the soil, of the roots,
Unfolding petals to behold—
We of the flower and the fruit,
We of the music we create.
We of this land that I now sing

"Holy Trinity"
Catholic
Church
Trinidad. Cal.

Entrust our poem to your ears:
This love and laughter I now bring.
The elder poets circle round,
And at last they nod their heads,
Assured their work has found an heir.
They bless me with their hands outspread

As my father blessed us always,
With every Sabbath, every week,
Old ritual, braided candle lit,
His hands on our heads, we stood meek.
The flame be quenched in a cup of wine.
I let him go, as I do Guy.

I count three stars in the heavens—
Fathers, brothers I sanctify.
Eternal song, receive to sing:
Poem, be my benediction.
Eternal journey, wander on.
From this sorrow I am shriven.

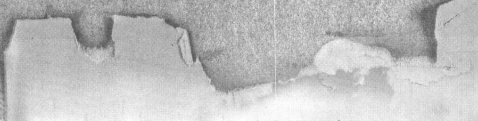

Details of Photographs

Page xii
Ericson. "Moonstone Beach at the Mouth of Little River with Hack." 1893. Westhaven, CA.
Boyle Collection. Comments: "Picture appeared in 'In the Redwood Realm,' published in
1893. Three men and hack (or buggy) included." HSU Photo ID: 1999.03.0478
http://library.humboldt.edu/humco/holdings/photodetail.php?S=1999.03.0478&CS=All%20
Collections&RS=ALL%20Regions&PS=Any%20Photographer&ST=ALL%20
words&SW=&C=1&R=0

Pages 2-3
Keir, Walter. "July 4th, Fortuna California" [Parade with Musicians and Automobiles Moving
Along the Street]. July 4, 1912. Fortuna, CA. Palmquist Collection. Comments: "Signs on
buildings read 'Friedenbach Bros.' and 'Theatre Trilma.'" HSU Photo ID: 2003.01.2117
{Partial Photo Used}
http://library.humboldt.edu/humco/holdings/photodetail.php?S=2003.01.2117&CS=All%20
Collections&RS=ALL%20Regions&PS=Any%20Photographer&ST=ALL%20
words&SW=&C=4&R=0

Pages 4-5
Britt, Peter. [Emil and Molli Britt Sit Along the Rogue River, and He Fishes]. Date Unknown.
Exact Location Unknown. Palmquist Collection. HSU Photo ID: 2003.01.1419 {Partial
Photo Used}
http://library.humboldt.edu/humco/holdings/photodetail.php?S=2003.01.1419&CS=All%20
Collections&RS=ALL%20Regions&PS=Any%20Photographer&ST=ALL%20
words&SW=&C=1&R=0

Pages 6-7
Unknown. "Fishing for Steelhead" [Fernbridge Fishing at Fernbridge]. Date Unknown.
Fernbridge, CA. Palmquist Collection. Comments: "Copy from Postcard. Eel River." HSU
Photo ID: 2003.01.0090 {Partial Photo Used}
http://library.humboldt.edu/humco/holdings/photodetail.php?S=2003.01.0090&CS=All%20
Collections&RS=ALL%20Regions&PS=Any%20Photographer&ST=ALL%20
words&SW=&C=1&R=0

Page 8
Fassold, Peter. [Baptism at Blue Lake (Mad River)] / [Women in White Being Baptized
Outdoors with a Group of Onlookers]. May, 1904. Blue Lake, CA. Palmquist Collection.
Comments: "Notes on verso regarding persons and events (baptism) in photo."
1999.07.0304 and 2003.01.1643 are the same. Blue Lake. HSU Photo ID: 2003.01.1643
http://library.humboldt.edu/humco/holdings/photodetail.php?S=2003.01.1643&CS=All%20
Collections&RS=ALL%20Regions&PS=Any%20Photographer&ST=ALL%20
words&SW=&C=2&R=1

Unknown. [Cemetery & Town]. Date Unknown. Ferndale, CA. Swanlund-Baker
Collection. Comments: "Supplemental information supplied by Ray Hillman, 2008:
region is Ferndale after 1901. The buildings in the background correspond to the area."
HSU Photo ID: 1999.01.0801 {Partial Photo Used}
http://library.humboldt.edu/humco/holdings/photodetail.
php?S=1999.01.0801&CS=All%20Collections&RS=ALL%20Regions&PS=Any%20
Photographer&ST=ALL%20words&SW=&C=1&R=0

Insert:
Ericson. "Jas. Greig's Stone Cutting Establishment, Eureka, California" / [Man with a
Hammer and Chisel Working on a Grave Stone]. Date Unknown. Eureka, CA. Palmquist
Collection. Comments: "'Albee' and 'Smith' are the names on grave stones." HSU Photo
ID: 2003.01.3283 {Partial Photo Used}
http://library.humboldt.edu/humco/holdings/photodetail.
php?S=2003.01.328&CS=All%20Collections&RS=ALL%20Regions&PS=Any%20
Photographer&ST=ALL%20words&SW=&C=11&R=3

Wax, William. [Geo Pate Crossing on Ferry at Scotia with His Two Horses Dexter and
Jumbo]. Date Unknown. Scotia, CA. Palmquist Collection. Comments: "Wm Wax photo
by comparison with other materials. 2003.01.2699 and .2700 are related, same person and
horses." HSU Photo ID: 2003.01.2700
http://library.humboldt.edu/humco/holdings/photodetail.
php?S=2003.01.2700&CS=All%20Collections&RS=ALL%20Regions&PS=Any%20
Photographer&ST=ALL%20words&SW=&C=1&R=0

Garrett, Edna M. [Three Women Sitting on a High Log in the Forest with Their Backs
Turned]. 1905. Exact Location Unknown. Palmquist Collection. HSU Photo ID:
2003.01.1908 {Partial Photo Used}
http://library.humboldt.edu/humco/holdings/photodetail.
php?S=2003.01.1908&CS=All%20Collections&RS=ALL%20Regions&PS=Any%20
Photographer&ST=ALL%20words&SW=&C=1&R=0

Ericson. [Man and Three Young Children Standing in the Forest]. Date Unknown. Exact
Location Unknown. Palmquist Collection. HSU Photo ID: 2003.01.3362 {Partial Photo
Used}
http://library.humboldt.edu/humco/holdings/photodetail.
php?S=2003.01.3362&CS=All%20Collections&RS=ALL%20Regions&PS=Any%20
Photographer&ST=ALL%20words&SW=&C=1&R=0

Page 18

Keir, Walter. "Horse Collar Tree, on Overland Road" / [Man Seated in the Knot of a Redwood Tree Reading a Newspaper]. Date Unknown. Southeastern Humboldt County, CA. Palmquist Collection. Comments: "P.M. 1914." HSU Photo ID: 2003.01.2138 {Partial Photo Used} http://library.humboldt.edu/humco/holdings/photodetail.php?S=2003.01.2138&CS=All%20 Collections&RS=ALL%20Regions&PS=Any%20Photographer&ST=ALL%20 words&SW=&C=1&R=0

Page 21

Unknown. [Grandmother Nellie Ruben, Martha Ruben Charles' Mother]. ~1937. Location Unknown. HCC Photos Collection. Comments: "'BE2' written in corner. Taken approx year 1937 age of Nellie Ruben 87. Tribe, Yurok, born in Weitchpec, California on June 27, 1849. Copied from original possession of, and thru courtesy of, Barbara Charles Eller." HSU Photo ID: 1999.07.3204 {Partial Photo Used} http://library.humboldt.edu/humco/holdings/photodetail.php?S=1999.07.3204&CS=All%20 Collections&RS=ALL%20Regions&PS=Any%20Photographer&ST=ALL%20 words&SW=&C=1&R=0

Page 22
Top:

Unknown. "Lumphy Pepper." 1923. Location Unspecified. Hover Collection. Comments: "Died 1929 when road was completed to Somes Bar. Cropped version of image in the Hover Collection of Karuk Baskets, p. 96: White Deerskin Dancer." HSU Photo ID: 1999.12.0006 {Partial Photo Used} http://library.humboldt.edu/humco/holdings/photodetail.php?S=1999.12.0006&CS=All%20 Collections&RS=ALL%20Regions&PS=Any%20Photographer&ST=ALL%20 words&SW=&C=1&R=0

Middle:

Wilson, Doug. [Pammy Risling and Lois Risling]. April, 1962. Within Humboldt County, CA. HCC Photos Collection. Comments: "Freshwater event described in the *Humboldt Times*. May 6, 1962; Titled: Children Meet Living History 'The Indians Were Real.'" HSU Photo ID: 1999.07.2937 {Partial Photo Used} http://library.humboldt.edu/humco/holdings/photodetail.php?S=1999.07.2937&CS=All%20 Collections&RS=ALL%20Regions&PS=Any%20Photographer&ST=ALL%20 words&SW=&C=1&R=0

Bottom:

Freeman, Emma Belle. [Bertha Stevens, Seated on a Beach in Between a Basket and a Bow with Arrows]. Date Unknown. Location Unspecified. Palmquist Collection. Comments: "Name identification from pp book *With Natures Children*, pg 107." HSU Photo ID: 2003.01.1862 {Partial Photo Used} http://library.humboldt.edu/humco/holdings/photodetail.php?S=2003.01.1862&CS=All%20 Collections&RS=ALL%20Regions&PS=Any%20Photographer&ST=ALL%20 words&SW=&C=1&R=0

Pages 24-25
Ericson. "A Glimpse of the Ocean, California/Coast Scene, Humboldt Co." Date
Unknown. Trinidad, CA. Ericson Collection. Comments: "'South Trinidad bay, Indian
Huts' is written on image." HSU Photo ID: 1999.02.0068 {Partial Photo Used}
http://library.humboldt.edu/humco/holdings/photodetail.
php?S=1999.02.0068&CS=All%20Collections&RS=ALL%20Regions&PS=Any%20
Photographer&ST=ALL%20words&SW=&C=2&R=0

Page 27
Wilson, Doug. [Yutish the Storyteller, Ernest Marshall]. April, 1962. Within Humboldt
County, CA. HCC Photos Collection. Comments: "Yut-ish the story teller, Ernest
Marshall Hoopa April 1962. Freshwater event described in the *Humboldt Times*. May 6,
1962; Titled: Children Meet Living History 'The Indians Were Real.'" HSU Photo ID:
1999.07.2939
http://library.humboldt.edu/humco/holdings/photodetail.
php?S=1999.07.2939&CS=All%20Collections&RS=ALL%20Regions&PS=Any%20
Photographer&ST=ALL%20words&SW=&C=1&R=0

Page 29
Palmquist, Peter E. "Rio Dell Bridge; Bridge Out" / [Parts of Bridge Still Standing, Other
Parts Washed Away]. December 23, 1964. Rio Dell, CA. Palmquist/Yale Collection.
Comments: "Rio Dell Bridge destroyed by 1962 flood." HSU Photo ID: 2012.02.0347
http://library.humboldt.edu/humco/holdings/photodetail.
php?S=2012.02.0347&CS=All%20Collections&RS=ALL%20Regions&PS=Any%20
Photographer&ST=ALL%20words&SW=&C=1&R=0

Page 30
Keir, Walter. "Rain Dampened Clothes, but Not Spirits, Big Bridge Celebration" / [People
Gathered in the Rain to Celebrate the Opening of Fernbridge]. November 16, 1911.
Fernbridge, CA. Palmquist Collection. HSU Photo ID: 2003.01.2131
http://library.humboldt.edu/humco/holdings/photodetail.
php?S=2003.01.2131&CS=All%20Collections&RS=ALL%20Regions&PS=Any%20
Photographer&ST=ALL%20words&SW=&C=1&R=0

Pages 32-33
Barber, Will Bradbury. [Group in Horse-pulled Wagon Amidst the Redwoods]. Date
Unknown. Location Unspecified. Palmquist Collection. Comments: "'W.B. Barber
Amateur Photographer Ferndale, Cal' (stamped on back of mount)." HSU Photo ID:
2003.01.1290
http://library.humboldt.edu/humco/holdings/photodetail.
php?S=2003.01.1290&CS=All%20Collections&RS=ALL%20Regions&PS=Any%20
Photographer&ST=ALL%20words&SW=&C=1&R=0

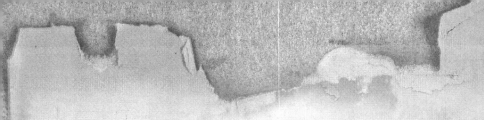

Page 34
Ericson. "Scene From Willow Creek, Near Berry's." Date Unknown. Willow Creek, CA.
Ericson Collection. Comments: "Looking west into Redwood Creek; Lord Ellis ridge and
Bald Mountain in background." HSU Photo ID: 1999.02.0090
http://library.humboldt.edu/humco/holdings/photodetail.
php?S=1999.02.0090&CS=All%20Collections&RS=ALL%20Regions&PS=Any%20
Photographer&ST=ALL%20words&SW=&C=2&R=0

Page 37
Baker, Ray Jerome. "Shelter Cove Pier." 1907? Shelter Cove, CA. Swanlund-Baker
Collection. HSU Photo ID: 1999.01.0294
http://library.humboldt.edu/humco/holdings/photodetail.
php?S=1999.01.0294&CS=All%20Collections&RS=ALL%20Regions&PS=Any%20
Photographer&ST=ALL%20words&SW=&C=1&R=0

Pages 38-39
Ericson. "Scene at Freshwater, Humboldt Co., California" / [Three Adults and Five Children
Gathered Around the Base of a Redwood Tree With a Large Split Up the Side]. Date
Unknown. Freshwater, CA. Palmquist Collection. Comments: "Sign on tree reads 'Hotel
Sequoia.'" HSU Photo ID: 2003.01.3044 {Partial Photo Used}
http://library.humboldt.edu/humco/holdings/photodetail.
php?S=2003.01.3044&CS=All%20Collections&RS=ALL%20Regions&PS=Any%20
Photographer&ST=ALL%20words&SW=&C=1&R=0

Page 40
Roberts, Ruth. [Native American Boy (Harry Roberts) and Older Woman (Alice Spott
Taylor) Standing Next to a River Holding up a Large Fish Catch]. Date Unknown. Location
Unspecified. Palmquist Collection. HSU Photo ID: 2003.01.2744 {Partial Photo Used}
http://library.humboldt.edu/humco/holdings/photodetail.
php?S=2003.01.2744&CS=All%20Collections&RS=ALL%20Regions&PS=Any%20
Photographer&ST=ALL%20words&SW=&C=1&R=0

Pages 42-43
Freeman, Art. "US Submarine. Samoa Beach, Humboldt Co. California" / [H-3 Submarine
on the Beach with People Gathered Around]. Date Unknown. Humboldt Bay, CA.
Palmquist Collection. HSU Photo ID: 2003.01.1764
http://library.humboldt.edu/humco/holdings/photodetail.php?R=40&S=samoa%20
beach&CS=All%20Collections&RS=ALL%20Regions&PS=Any%20
Photographer&ST=ALL%20words&SW=&C=44

Pages 44-45
Meiser, J.A. [Chinese Leaving Eureka] / [Group of People on a Barge]. 1906. Humboldt
Bay, CA. Palmquist Collection. Comments: "Yacht Club in background." HSU Photo ID:
2003.01.2312

http://library.humboldt.edu/humco/holdings/photodetail.
php?S=2003.01.2312&CS=All%20Collections&RS=ALL%20Regions&PS=Any%20
Photographer&ST=ALL%20words&SW=&C=1&R=0

Pages 46-47
Ericson. "Scene At Samoa, Eureka, Humboldt Co., California" / [View from the Shore
Looking at the Side of a Pier That Extends into Humboldt Bay]. 1893? Humboldt Bay,
CA. Palmquist Collection. Comments: "Sign on building next to pier reads 'Baths.'"
HSU Photo ID: 2003.01.3107
http://library.humboldt.edu/humco/holdings/photodetail.
php?S=2003.01.3107&CS=All%20Collections&RS=ALL%20Regions&PS=Any%20
Photographer&ST=ALL%20words&SW=&C=1&R=0

Page 48
Top:
Baker, Ray Jerome. [Young Boys Holding Photograph Prints in Lumber Yard/Sawmill].
Date Unknown. Location Unspecified. Palmquist Collection. HSU Photo ID:
2003.01.0234
http://library.humboldt.edu/humco/holdings/photodetail.
php?S=2003.01.0234&CS=All%20Collections&RS=ALL%20Regions&PS=Any%20
Photographer&ST=ALL%20words&SW=&C=1&R=0
Middle:
Britt, Peter. [Group Portrait at Sawmill]. Date Unknown. Location Unspecified. Palmquist
Collection. HSU Photo ID: 2003.01.1415
http://library.humboldt.edu/humco/holdings/photodetail.
php?S=2003.01.1415&CS=All%20Collections&RS=ALL%20Regions&PS=Any%20
Photographer&ST=ALL%20words&SW=&C=1&R=0
Bottom:
Ericson. [Augustus William Ericson with Arms Crossed Leaning Against a Large Redwood
Stump]. Date Unknown. Freshwater, CA. Palmquist Collection. HSU Photo ID:
2003.01.3030
http://library.humboldt.edu/humco/holdings/photodetail.
php?S=2003.01.3030&CS=All%20Collections&RS=ALL%20Regions&PS=Any%20
Photographer&ST=ALL%20words&SW=&C=1&R=0

Page 51
Unknown. [Fieldbrook or Blue Lake Saloon Interior]. Date Unknown. Fieldbrook or Blue
Lake, CA. HCC Photos Collection. Comments: "'Courtesy Hazel Curpill (?) 1972' on
verso." HSU Photo ID: 1999.07.1724
http://library.humboldt.edu/humco/holdings/photodetail.
php?S=1999.07.1724&CS=All%20Collections&RS=ALL%20Regions&PS=Any%20
Photographer&ST=ALL%20words&SW=&C=1&R=0

Page 52
Freeman, Art. "Arcata Fair, 1919" / [Exhibit Featuring Flowers at Arcata Fair, 1919]. 1919. Arcata, CA. HCC Photos Collection. Comments: "Presented to library by Joanne Beer Mace Fall 1967." HSU Photo ID: 1999.07.0056 {Partial Photo Used}
http://library.humboldt.edu/humco/holdings/photodetail.php?S=1999.07.0056%20 &CS=All%20Collections&RS=ALL%20Regions&PS=Any%20Photographer&ST=ALL%20 words&SW=&C=1&R=0

Page 55
Unknown. [Arcata Plaza Celebration with Band]. April, 2, 1870? Arcata, CA. HCC Photos Collection. Comments: "Arcata Plaza 2 April 1870? Charles Wallace Jacob Johnson. 'HT 30 April 1870 p.3 col.2' on verso." HSU Photo ID: 1999.07.0113 {Partial Photo Used}
http://library.humboldt.edu/humco/holdings/photodetail. php?S=1999.07.0113&CS=All%20Collections&RS=ALL%20Regions&PS=Any%20 Photographer&ST=ALL%20words&SW=&C=1&R=0

Page 56
Dunklin, Thomas B. "Elk & Egret." 2009. Big Lagoon, CA. Comments: "Herd of elk and one egret standing in channel in Big Lagoon."
For more info on Thomas B. Dunklin's work see: www.vimeo.com/todu

Pages 56- 57
Faded Background Photo:
Boyle, Katie. "An Unknown Photographer Trying To Get a Closer Picture of Elk Herd at Gold Bluff Beach." 1969. Orick, CA. Boyle Collection. HSU Photo ID: 1999.03.0490 {Partial Photo Used & Reversed}
http://library.humboldt.edu/humco/holdings/photodetail. php?S=1999.03.0490&CS=All%20Collections&RS=ALL%20Regions&PS=Any%20 Photographer&ST=ALL%20words&SW=&C=1&R=0

Page 58
Unknown. [Musician Visited By Ghost; Spirit Photography]. 1874 or earlier. Location Unspecified. Palmquist Collection. Comments: "Printed on photo left border, 'Entered according to Act of Congress, in the year 1874, by Melander + Bro. Chicago, in the Office of the Librarian of Congress at Washington.' Spirit Photography." HSU Photo ID: 2003.01.0300
http://library.humboldt.edu/humco/holdings/photodetail.php?S=Musician%20 visited%20by%20ghost&CS=All%20Collections&RS=ALL%20Regions&PS=Any%20 Photographer&ST=ALL%20words&SW=&C=1&R=0

Pages 60-61
Unknown. "Catching Salmon Near Korbel" / [Fish Dam/Weir Stretching Across Stream]. 1890 or earlier. Korbel, CA. Palmquist Collection. Comments: "c.1890 or earlier." HSU Photo ID: 2003.01.0239 {Partial Photo Used}

http://library.humboldt.edu/humco/holdings/photodetail.
php?S=2003.01.0239&CS=All%20Collections&RS=ALL%20Regions&PS=Any%20
Photographer&ST=ALL%20words&SW=&C=1&R=0

Page 62
Top:
Unknown. "Weitchpec Post Office." 1919. Weitchpec, CA. Boyle Collection.
HSU Photo ID: 1999.03.0896
http://library.humboldt.edu/humco/holdings/photodetail.
php?R=3&S=weitchpec&CS=All%20Collections&RS=ALL%20Regions&PS=Any%20
Photographer&ST=ALL%20words&SW=&C=33

Bottom:
Unknown. "Weitchpec" / [Bird's Eye View of Weitchpec and Rivers]. Date Unknown.
Weitchpec, CA. Palmquist Collection. HSU Photo ID: 2003.01.0608
http://library.humboldt.edu/humco/holdings/photodetail.
php?S=2003.01.0608&CS=All%20Collections&RS=ALL%20Regions&PS=Any%20
Photographer&ST=ALL%20words&SW=&C=1&R=0

Page 64
Ericson. [Bendixsen Ship Yard - "Jane Stanford" Just Launched Unknown]. 1892.
Humboldt Bay, CA. Ericson Collection. HSU Photo ID: 1999.02.0278
http://library.humboldt.edu/humco/holdings/photodetail.
php?R=0&S=1999.02.0278&CS=All%20Collections&RS=ALL%20
Regions&PS=Any%20Photographer&ST=ALL%20words&SW=&C=2

Pages 66-67
Swett, Martin. "Sunday Evening Rain Walk." 2004. Dry Lagoon, CA.
For more information see: https://www.flickr.com/photos/25974668@N06/5378298933/
in/dateposted/

Page 68
Freeman, Emma Belle. [Native American Man Posing Next to a Canoe on the
Riverbank]. Date Unknown. Location Unspecified. Palmquist Collection. Comments:
"Name identification from pp book, *With Natures Children*, pg 116." HSU Photo ID:
2003.01.1826
http://library.humboldt.edu/humco/holdings/photodetail.php?S=Native%20
American%20Posing%20Next%20To%20a%20Canoe&CS=All%20
Collections&RS=ALL%20Regions&PS=Any%20Photographer&ST=ALL%20
words&SW=&C=9&R=1

Page 70
McGraw, Nellie Tichenor. "A Warm Day" / [Children Relax at the Side of a River, Some
Standing in Water]. Date Unknown. Hoopa, CA. Palmquist/Yale Collection. Comments:
"Nellie McGraw (Hedgpeth) photo album." HSU Photo ID: 2012.02.0732

http://library.humboldt.edu/humco/holdings/photodetail.
php?S=2012.02.0732&CS=All%20Collections&RS=ALL%20Regions&PS=Any%20
Photographer&ST=ALL%20words&SW=&C=1&R=0

Page 72
Freeman, Emma Belle. "The Water Falls, Hoopa Cal." / [Native American Woman Gesturing Towards a Waterfall]. Date Unknown. Location Unspecified, but thought to be Hoopa, CA. Palmquist Collection. HSU Photo ID: 2003.01.1830
http://library.humboldt.edu/humco/holdings/photodetail.php?S=The%20
Water%20Falls&CS=All%20Collections&RS=ALL%20Regions&PS=Any%20
Photographer&ST=ALL%20words&SW=&C=2&R=0

Pages 74-75
Swett, Martin. "Oak Above Fog, Dyersville Loop." January 2001. Southern Humboldt, CA. {Partial Photo Used}
For more information see: https://www.flickr.com/photos/25974668@N06/2460412565/in/
dateposted/

Page 76
Unknown. "Trinidad Holy Trinity Catholic Church in Disrepair." Date Unknown. Trinidad, CA. Boyle Collection. HSU Photo ID: 1999.03.0768
http://library.humboldt.edu/humco/holdings/photodetail.php?S=Trinidad%20Holy%20
Trinity%20Catholic&CS=All%20Collections&RS=ALL%20Regions&PS=Any%20
Photographer&ST=ALL%20words&SW=&C=3&R=0

Page 79
Dunklin, Thomas B. "Chinook from Below." 2011. Middle Fork of the Smith River, CA. Comments: "Underwater view of Chinook salmon, viewed from below, backlit by sun, with view of riparian foliage."
For more info on Thomas B. Dunklin's work see: www.vimeo.com/todu